THE JPS B'NAI MITZVAH TORAH COMMENTARY

Shofetim (Deuteronomy 16:18–21:9)
Haftarah (Isaiah 51:12–52:12)

Rabbi Jeffrey K. Salkin

The Jewish Publication Society · Philadelphia
University of Nebraska Press · Lincoln

INTRODUCTION

News flash: the most important thing about becoming bar or bat mitzvah isn't the party. Nor is it the presents. Nor even being able to celebrate with your family and friends—as wonderful as those things are. Nor is it even standing before the congregation and reading the prayers of the liturgy—as important as that is.

No, the most important thing about becoming bar or bat mitzvah is sharing Torah with the congregation. And why is that? Because of all Jewish skills, that is the most important one.

Here is what is true about rites of passage: you can tell what a culture values by the tasks it asks its young people to perform on their way to maturity. In American culture, you become responsible for driving, responsible for voting, and yes, responsible for drinking responsibly.

In some cultures, the rite of passage toward maturity includes some kind of trial, or a test of strength. Sometimes, it is a kind of "outward bound" camping adventure. Among the Maasai tribe in Africa, it is traditional for a young person to hunt and kill a lion. In some Hispanic cultures, fifteen year-old girls celebrate the *quinceañera*, which marks their entrance into maturity.

What is Judaism's way of marking maturity? It combines both of these rites of passage: *responsibility* and *test*. You show that you are on your way to becoming a *responsible* Jewish adult through a public *test* of strength and knowledge—reading or chanting Torah, and then teaching it to the congregation.

This is the most important Jewish ritual mitzvah (commandment), and that is how you demonstrate that you are, truly, bar or bat mitzvah—old enough to be responsible for the mitzvot.

What Is Torah?

So, what exactly is the Torah? You probably know this already, but let's review.

The Torah (teaching) consists of "the five books of Moses," sometimes also called the *chumash* (from the Hebrew word *chameish,* which means "five"), or, sometimes, the Greek word Pentateuch (which means "the five teachings").

Here are the five books of the Torah, with their common names and their Hebrew names.

> **Genesis (The beginning), which in Hebrew is Bere'shit (from the first words—"When God began to create").** Bere'shit spans the years from Creation to Joseph's death in Egypt. Many of the Bible's best stories are in Genesis: the creation story itself; Adam and Eve in the Garden of Eden; Cain and Abel; Noah and the Flood; and the tales of the Patriarchs and Matriarchs, Abraham, Isaac, Jacob, Sarah, Rebekah, Rachel, and Leah. It also includes one of the greatest pieces of world literature, the story of Joseph, which is actually the oldest complete novel in history, comprising more than one-quarter of all Genesis.

> **Exodus (Getting out), which in Hebrew is Shemot (These are the names).** Exodus begins with the story of the Israelite slavery in Egypt. It then moves to the rise of Moses as a leader, and the Israelites' liberation from slavery. After the Israelites leave Egypt, they experience the miracle of the parting of the Sea of Reeds (or "Red Sea"); the giving of the Ten Commandments at Mount Sinai; the idolatry of the Golden Calf; and the design and construction of the Tabernacle and of the ark for the original tablets of the law, which our ancestors carried with them in the desert. Exodus also includes various ethical and civil laws, such as "You shall not wrong a stranger or oppress him, for you were strangers in the land of Egypt" (22:20).

> **Leviticus (about the Levites), or, in Hebrew, Va-yikra' (And God called).** It goes into great detail about the kinds of sacrifices that the ancient Israelites brought as offerings; the laws of ritual purity; the animals that were permitted and forbidden for eating (the beginnings of the tradition of kashrut, the Jewish dietary laws); the diagnosis of various skin diseases; the ethical laws of holiness; the ritual calendar of the Jewish year; and various agricultural laws concerning the treatment of the Land of Israel. Leviticus is basically the manual of ancient Judaism.

➤ **Numbers (because the book begins with the census of the Israelites), or, in Hebrew, Be-midbar (In the wilderness).** The book
describes the forty years of wandering in the wilderness and the
various rebellions against Moses. The constant theme: "Egypt
wasn't so bad. Maybe we should go back." The greatest rebellion
against Moses was the negative reports of the spies about the
Land of Israel, which discouraged the Israelites from wanting to
move forward into the land. For that reason, the "wilderness generation" must die off before a new generation can come into maturity and finish the journey.

➤ **Deuteronomy (The repetition of the laws of the Torah), or, in
Hebrew, Devarim (The words).** The final book of the Torah is,
essentially, Moses's farewell address to the Israelites as they pre-
pare to enter the Land of Israel. Here we find various laws that
had been previously taught, though sometimes with different
wording. Much of Deuteronomy contains laws that will be important to the Israelites as they enter the Land of Israel—laws
concerning the establishment of a monarchy and the ethics of
warfare. Perhaps the most famous passage from Deuteronomy
contains the *Shema,* the declaration of God's unity and unique-
ness, and the *Ve-ahavta,* which follows it. Deuteronomy ends with
the death of Moses on Mount Nebo as he looks across the Jordan
Valley into the land that he will not enter.

Jews read the Torah in sequence—starting with Bere'shit right after Simchat Torah in the autumn, and then finishing Devarim on the
following Simchat Torah. Each Torah portion is called a parashah (di-
vision; sometimes called a *sidrah,* a place in the order of the Torah
reading). The stories go around in a full circle, reminding us that we
can always gain more insights and more wisdom from the Torah. This
means that if you don't "get" the meaning this year, don't worry—it
will come around again.

And What Else? The Haftarah

We read or chant the Torah from the Torah scroll—the most sacred
thing that a Jewish community has in its possession. The Torah is

written without vowels, and the ability to read it and chant it is part of the challenge and the test.

But there is more to the synagogue reading. Every Torah reading has an accompanying haftarah reading. Haftarah means "conclusion," because there was once a time when the service actually ended with that reading. Some scholars believe that the reading of the haftarah originated at a time when non-Jewish authorities outlawed the reading of the Torah, and the Jews read the haftarah sections instead. In fact, in some synagogues, young people who become bar or bat mitzvah read very little Torah and instead read the entire haftarah portion.

The haftarah portion comes from the Nevi'im, the prophetic books, which are the second part of the Jewish Bible. It is either read or chanted from a Hebrew Bible, or maybe from a booklet or a photocopy.

The ancient sages chose the haftarah passages because their themes reminded them of the words or stories in the Torah text. Sometimes, they chose *haftarah* with special themes in honor of a festival or an upcoming festival.

Not all books in the prophetic section of the Hebrew Bible consist of prophecy. Several are historical. For example:

The book of Joshua tells the story of the conquest and settlement of Israel.

The book of Judges speaks of the period of early tribal rulers who would rise to power, usually for the purpose of uniting the tribes in war against their enemies. Some of these leaders are famous: Deborah, the great prophetess and military leader, and Samson, the biblical strong man.

The books of Samuel start with Samuel, the last judge, and then move to the creation of the Israelite monarchy under Saul and David (approximately 1000 BCE).

The books of Kings tell of the death of King David, the rise of King Solomon, and how the Israelite kingdom split into the Northern Kingdom of Israel and the Southern Kingdom of Judah (approximately 900 BCE).

And then there are the books of the prophets, those spokesmen for God whose words fired the Jewish conscience. Their names are immortal: Isaiah, Jeremiah, Ezekiel, Amos, Hosea, among others.

Someone once said: "There is no evidence of a biblical prophet ever being invited back a second time for dinner." Why? Because the prophets were tough. They had no patience for injustice, apathy, or hypocrisy. No one escaped their criticisms. Here's what they taught:

› God commands the Jews to behave decently toward one another. In fact, God cares more about basic ethics and decency than about ritual behavior.

› God chose the Jews *not* for special privileges, but for special duties to humanity.

› As bad as the Jews sometimes were, there was always the possibility that they would improve their behavior.

› As bad as things might be now, it will not always be that way. Someday, there will be universal justice and peace. Human history is moving forward toward an ultimate conclusion that some call the Messianic Age: a time of universal peace and prosperity for the Jewish people and for all the people of the world.

Your Mission—To Teach Torah to the Congregation

On the day when you become bar or bat mitzvah, you will be reading, or chanting, Torah—in Hebrew. You will be reading, or chanting, the haftarah—in Hebrew. That is the major skill that publicly marks the becoming of bar or bat mitzvah. But, perhaps even more important than that, you need to be able to teach something about the Torah portion, and perhaps the haftarah as well.

And that is where this book comes in. It will be a very valuable resource for you, and your family, in the b'nai mitzvah process.

Here is what you will find in it:

› A brief **summary** of every Torah portion. This is a basic overview of the portion; and, while it might not refer to everything in the Torah portion, it will explain its most important aspects.

› A list of the **major ideas** in the Torah portion. The purpose: to make the Torah portion real, in ways that we can relate to. Every Torah portion contains unique ideas, and when you put all of those ideas together, you actually come up with a list of Judaism's most important ideas.

> Two **divrei Torah** ("words of Torah," or "sermonettes") for each portion. These *divrei Torah* explain significant aspects of the Torah portion in accessible, reader-friendly language. Each *devar Torah* contains references to **traditional** Jewish sources (those that were written before the modern era), as well as **modern** sources and quotes. We have searched, far and wide, to find sources that are unusual, interesting, and not just the "same old stuff" that many people already know about the Torah portion. Why did we include these minisermons in the volume? Not because we want you to simply copy those sermons and pass them off as your own (that would be cheating), though you are free to quote from them. We included them so that you can see what is possible—how you can try to make meaning for yourself out of the words of Torah.

> **Connections:** This is perhaps the most valuable part. It's a list of questions that you can ask yourself, or that others might help you think about—any of which can lead to the creation of your *devar Torah.*

Note: you don't have to like everything that's in a particular Torah portion. Some aren't that loveable. Some are hard to understand; some are about religious practices that people today might find confusing, and even offensive; some contain ideas that we might find totally outmoded.

But this doesn't have to get in the way. After all, most kids spend a lot of time thinking about stories that contain ideas that modern people would find totally bizarre. Any good medieval fantasy story falls into that category.

And we also believe that, if you spend just a little bit of time with those texts, you can begin to understand what the author was trying to say.

This volume goes one step further. Sometimes, the haftarah comes off as a second thought, and no one really thinks about it. We have tried to solve that problem by including a **summary** of each haftarah, and then a mini-sermon on the haftarah. This will help you learn how these sacred words are relevant to today's world, and even to your own life.

All Bible quotations come from the NJPS translation, which is found in the many different editions of the JPS TANAKH; in the Conservative movement's *Etz Hayim: Torah and Commentary;* in the Reform movement's *Torah: A Modern Commentary;* and in other Bible commentaries and study guides.

How Do I Write a *Devar Torah?*

It really is easier than it looks.

There are many ways of thinking about the *devar Torah*. It is, of course, a short sermon on the meaning of the Torah (and, perhaps, the haftarah) portion. It might even be helpful to think of the *devar Torah* as a "book report" on the portion itself.

The most important thing you can know about this sacred task is: *Learn* the words. *Love* the words. Teach people what it could mean to *live* the words.

Here's a basic outline for a *devar Torah*:

"My Torah portion is (name of portion) _____,
   from the book of _____ , chapter

   _____.
"In my Torah portion, we learn that_____
   (Summary of portion)
"For me, the most important lesson of this Torah portion is (what
   is the best thing in the portion? Take the portion as a whole;
   your *devar Torah* does not have to be only, or specifically, on the
   verses that you are reading).
"As I learned my Torah portion, I found myself wondering:
   ➤ *Raise a question that the Torah portion itself raises.*
   ➤ *"Pick a fight" with the portion. Argue with it.*
   ➤ *Answer a question* that is listed in the "Connections" section of
      each Torah portion.
   ➤ *Suggest a question to your rabbi* that you would want the rabbi
      to answer in his or her own *devar Torah* or sermon.

"I have lived the values of the Torah by _____
(here, you can talk about how the Torah portion relates to your
own life. If you have done a mitzvah project, you can talk about
that here).

How To Keep It from Being Boring
(and You from Being Bored)

Some people just don't like giving traditional speeches. From our per-
spective, that's really okay. Perhaps you can teach Torah in a different
way—one that makes sense to you.

> - Write an "open letter" to one of the characters in your Torah por-
>   tion. "Dear Abraham: I hope that your trip to Canaan was not too
>   hard . . ." "Dear Moses: Were you afraid when you got the Ten
>   Commandments on Mount Sinai? I sure would have been . . ."
> - Write a news story about what happens. Imagine yourself to
>   be a television or news reporter. "Residents of neighboring cit-
>   ies were horrified yesterday as the wicked cities of Sodom and
>   Gomorrah were burned to the ground. Some say that God was
>   responsible . . ."
> - Write an imaginary interview with a character in your Torah portion.
> - Tell the story from the point of view of another character, or a mi-
>   nor character, in the story. For instance, tell the story of the Gar-
>   den of Eden from the point of view of the serpent. Or the story
>   of the Binding of Isaac from the point of view of the ram, which
>   was substituted for Isaac as a sacrifice. Or perhaps the story of
>   the sale of Joseph from the point of view of his coat, which was
>   stripped off him and dipped in a goat's blood.
> - Write a poem about your Torah portion.
> - Write a song about your Torah portion.
> - Write a play about your Torah portion, and have some friends act
>   it out with you.
> - Create a piece of artwork about your Torah portion.

The bottom line is: Make this a joyful experience. Yes—it could
even be fun.

The Very Last Thing You Need to Know at This Point

The Torah scroll is written without vowels. Why? Don't *sofrim* (Torah scribes) know the vowels?

Of course they do.

So, why do they leave the vowels out?

One reason is that the Torah came into existence at a time when sages were still arguing about the proper vowels, and the proper pronunciation.

But here is another reason: The Torah text, as we have it today, and as it sits in the scroll, is actually *an unfinished work*. Think of it: the words are just sitting there. Because they have no vowels, it is as if they have no voice.

When we read the Torah publicly, we give voice to the ancient words. And when we find meaning in those ancient words, and we talk about those meanings, those words jump to life. They enter our lives. They make our world deeper and better.

Mazal tov to you, and your family. This is your journey toward Jewish maturity. Love it.

THE TORAH

❖ Shofetim: Deuteronomy 16:18–21:9

Shofetim deals mostly with the administration of justice. The Israelites are commanded to appoint judges and civic officials.

In addition, the Torah portion talks about the way that Israelite kings are supposed to behave—not unlimited in power, as in other ancient and even modern monarchies, but humble and obedient to the Torah.

Finally, the Israelite method of doing justice must extend to the way that the Israelites will fight wars to conquer the Land of Israel.

Summary

> - The Israelites are commanded to appoint "magistrates and officials," who are commanded to be impartial in judgment and not to accept bribes. (16:18–20)
> - The penalty for worshiping idols is death, but the death penalty can be given only if there are two or more witnesses to the act. (17:2–7)
> - The Israelites are permitted to have a king, but there are limits to what that king can do. He must be a fellow Israelite, and he is forbidden to have many horses, wives, or wealth. In addition, the king must write a copy of the Torah and must have it with him at all times. (17:14–20)
> - The Israelites are forbidden to engage in the ritual practices of the Canaanites who dwell in the Land of Israel: sacrificing children, engaging in various magical practices, and attempting to communicate with the dead. (18:9–14)
> - There are specific laws for the way that wars to conquer the Land of Israel are to be fought and rules for who shall be released from battle. Those who were just starting out in life—building a new house, planting crops, or preparing to get married—are exempt from going to war. So, too, there are specific laws for the way that an Israelite army is to behave in war, first and foremost by offering terms of peace to its enemies, killing only the males who fight, and not destroying trees. (20:1–20)

The Big Ideas

> **Judaism introduces the idea of a just society.** How the Bible defines a just society is so powerful that it deeply influenced the development of American justice. Deuteronomy imagines a society where justice is impartial, blind to social position, and immune to bribery. The traditional American symbol of justice—a blindfolded woman holding equal scales—reminds us of this biblical ideal.

> **Human life is sacred.** We are free to disagree with the severity of the death penalty for worshiping idols—or any crime, for that matter. But the Torah is making a valuable point: the death penalty is such a grievous and extreme punishment that it cannot be administered lightly. The court must be absolutely sure of the crime that has been committed, and that assurance can only come when there is a minimum of two witnesses.

> **Leadership is service, not power or status.** That is the reason why the Torah puts so many limitations on kings and what they are permitted to do—so that the king will treat his subjects with dignity and not have too much power.

> **The Jews must be different from other people.** This is the essential lesson behind many of the Torah's laws—to ensure that the People of Israel will be an *am kadosh* (holy people). In this particular context, however, it means that the Israelites must reject the ritual elements of the Canaanite religion. It is interesting to note that most of those practices are connected to death—the ritual offering of children, and attempting to speak to the dead. By rejecting those practices, Judaism guaranteed that it would become a religion that celebrates life, not one that glorifies death.

> **There is a "right" way to fight wars.** Judaism has always rejected the idea that "war is hell" and that soldiers can do whatever they want to do. The Torah lists specific prohibitions on who can fight a war (and who doesn't have to fight), and how to fight a war. For many centuries, when the Jews did not have their own sovereign state, these rules were theoretical. In the modern State of Israel, these rules have new life, and form the basis for the Israeli notion of *tohar ha-neshek*, "purity of arms," which is part of the standard operating procedure for the Israel Defense Forces.

Divrei Torah

KINGS: GOOD OR BAD?

To quote the famous Jewish comedian Mel Brooks: "It's good to be king." Well, sort of.

There aren't that many kings and queens in the contemporary world. While there are still many countries that have royalty (the United Kingdom, the Netherlands, Norway, Sweden, and Saudi Arabia, for example), in many cases, they don't rule. Their countries are constitutional monarchies, which means that there are democratically elected officials, like prime ministers. Being a king or queen is largely ceremonial and symbolic.

But in the ancient world, and right up to the modern era, kings had absolute power of life and death over their subjects, and they could do anything they wanted. As the Israeli scholar Menachem Lorberbaum has written: "In the ancient Near East, the king was believed to be 'the image of God.' In ancient Egypt, the king himself was a god. In ancient Greece, the king had a special relationship with God. Roman emperors referred to themselves as sons of God." The king and only the king was in the image of God. No one else. Talk about power! (Notice how Judaism changed that, and said that all people are made in God's image.)

Deuteronomy changed the entire way that royalty would govern. They had to follow certain rules. The king cannot have a lot of horses, and cannot send people back to Egypt to get them. He cannot have multiple wives. He cannot amass huge riches. The king must write a Torah (or, perhaps just the book of Deuteronomy). The king is not the author of the laws but a student of the laws.

The king cannot be on a "power trip." Maimonides writes: "The king must not exercise his authority in a 'stuck up' manner. He should deal graciously and compassionately with the small and the great, conduct the people's affairs in their best interests, be wary of the honor of even the lowliest. When he addresses the public, he should use gentle language."

This is all good. Except, centuries later, the "wise" King Solomon forgot those laws. 1 Kings 10:21 says that all his vessels were of gold. Well, there goes the rule against amassing great wealth. Solomon had chariots and horses—which he got from Egypt! And as for wives, even

Solomon probably didn't know how many wives he had. All of Deuteronomy's rules went out the window.

Solomon enslaved his people in order to build garrison cities. Sound familiar? That is how the ancient Israelites became slaves in Egypt! Solomon became like a Pharaoh! And what happens after Solomon dies? His son becomes king, decides to run things even worse than Solomon did, and the kingdom falls apart.

Mel Brooks might have been right. It might have been "good to be king." But, like everything in Judaism, you have to know your limits as well. Solomon didn't, and look what happened. And look what else has happened when kings and modern-day rulers exercise total power. It never turns out well. So unless a ruler doesn't just look good or sound good, but is truly good, watch out.

WAR IS HELL

That was what an old movie claimed.

The Torah might not go that far, but it requires something of the Israelites that no other ancient people does. It constrains war. Among other things, you have to offer a besieged city terms of peace (20:10), and you cannot destroy fruit-bearing trees (2:19–20). This last point is very important; it would mean that it is wrong to use defoliants (chemicals that will destroy trees and plant life).

The Jewish ideal is peace. Numerous texts and prayers insist that we always pursue peace. A midrash teaches: "Peace is a great thing, for even during war peace is necessary. . . . Great is peace, for God created no fairer attribute than that of peace, which has been given to the righteous. Great is peace, for it was given as a reward for devotion to Torah and good deeds."

What about today? How do we make that vision real? And how do we constrain our actions when we do wage war?

Moshe Halbertal, an important Israeli thinker, teaches about the idea of *tohar ha-neshek,* "the purity of arms," and has written a code of conduct that was adopted by the Israel Defense Forces. He teaches that every soldier should ask himself or herself these questions before engaging in any action:

- ➤ Are my actions necessary?
- ➤ Am I targeting only those who are combatants? Am I doing everything possible as a soldier to avoid harming civilians—even to the point of risking my own safety? Are my actions proportionate to the danger that I am facing?

This doesn't mean that if the enemy kills only three of your soldiers, you are allowed to kill only three of theirs. In fact, you can kill as many combatants as you have to in order to make them stop killing. Proportionality only applies to the possible danger that noncombatants might face.

Are these ideas too idealistic? Perhaps. But it is the true Jewish way to be idealistic and to put forward ideas that many people might not yet accept, but which are still necessary.

These issues are very real today. Sadly, the United States still fights wars, and so does Israel. Morality in war might be difficult, but it is a goal that is necessary to strive for. As Professor Halbertal has said: "My children and their friends want to come back from their military duty, and they want to be able to look at themselves in the mirror."

Connections

› Why is it so important to have two or three witnesses to a crime, rather than just one?

› How do you define "justice"? Why is justice so important to God and to humanity? Is this a just world? How can you make it more just?

› Have you ever felt like a victim of injustice? How did you react?

› Do you agree that there should be rules for the way wars are fought? What are some reasons why such rules would be unnecessary or ineffective? Do such rules apply to other areas of life where there are conflicts? What other rules should there be for war?

THE HAFTARAH

❖ Shofetim: Isaiah 51:12–52:12

It hasn't been enough for the prophet, known as Second Isaiah, to issue promises of the future redemption of the Jewish people. No, God must comfort the people directly. That is why this haftarah begins with the words "I, I am He who comforts you!" (51:12). It's as if the people have forgotten all about God, and God jumps in and reminds them of who God really is.

Interesting to note: God does not identify the Divine Self as the One who, centuries ago, took them out of Egypt. God does not remind them of the giving of the Ten Commandments (though the first word of this haftarah—*Anokhi*—"I am"—is an echo of the first words of the Ten Commandments).

No, God instead reminds the Jews of the creation story. God is the one "who stretched out the skies and made firm the earth!" (51:13). This is a major theme for the prophet Second Isaiah. Here's why: The Jews who were living in exile in Babylonia might have been tempted to believe that the Babylonian gods were responsible for the Creation. God (or at least the prophet) is afraid of competition between the Egyptian gods and God and therefore has to reassert that God alone was the Creator. For that reason, Second Isaiah is sometimes credited with originating the idea of monotheism—that only God is God, and that the so-called other gods don't even exist.

It's not as if God has totally forgotten the Exodus from Egypt. Hardly. When the Israelites left Egypt, how did they do it? "Hurriedly" (Exod. 12:11); that was why they left Egypt without time for their bread to rise. But there is about to be a new "exodus"; this time, it will be the Jews leaving exile in Babylonia. This new "exodus" from Babylonia will not be like the first Exodus. "For you will not depart in haste, nor will you leave in flight; for the Lord is marching before you, the God of Israel is your rear guard" (Isa. 52:12). God is with the Jews. There is no need to fear.

Jerusalem or Zion?

If someone were to ask you to identify the twin cities, you would probably say Minneapolis and Saint Paul, Minnesota.

It turns out that Jerusalem is also a twin city. There are two Jerusalems. You could figure that out grammatically, because the Hebrew word for Jerusalem—*Yerushalayim*—is actually in the plural form.

Today some people see two Jerusalems in that Jerusalem has an old, walled city, and a new, modern city. Others looks at East Jerusalem, which is predominately Arab, and West Jerusalem, which is predominately Jewish. But there is another way to look at the two Jerusalems; the haftarah constantly refers to the holy city as both "Zion" and "Jerusalem."

Is there a difference between "Zion" and "Jerusalem," or are they simply synonyms for the same place? Rabbis W. Gunther Plaut and Chaim Stern teach: "'Zion' and 'Jerusalem' express two aspects of the city. Zion was predominantly its spiritual identification, and Jerusalem its geographic aspect."

This is crucial to understanding Jerusalem—and probably to understanding the entire State of Israel. There is a geographic reality to the city, but there is also a spiritual reality. Or, think of it this way: In "Jerusalem" there are shopping malls. In "Zion" there are synagogues and yeshivas.

For the ancient Rabbis, it sometimes seemed as if the spiritual Jerusalem had become more important than the "real" Jerusalem. We can understand why; some of those Rabbis were writing after the Romans had destroyed Jerusalem, and they were carrying a sacred memory within their hearts. They liked to imagine that there was a *Yerushalayim shel matah,* an earthly Jerusalem, a Jerusalem of reality—as well as a *Yerushalayim shel ma'alah,* a heavenly Jerusalem, a Jerusalem of the ideal. Zion is the heavenly ideal. Jerusalem is the earthly reality.

What is the heavenly Jerusalem like? The ancient sages imagined Jerusalem to be a place of miracles: "No man ever had an accident in Jerusalem; no fire ever broke out in Jerusalem; no man ever said, 'There is no place for me to sleep in Jerusalem.'" It's the kind of place we wish for in our dreams.

Yes, there is something magical about Jerusalem—a magic that, for the Jew, exists nowhere else on earth. There is a special atmosphere in Jerusalem that some describe as otherworldly. But while it's wonderful to sense that specialness, let's not get carried away. Jerusalem, and all of Israel, is a very real place, with very real problems and challenges. "Zion" might be the uniquely spiritual aspect of Jerusalem, but there is still "Jerusalem" the capital, with all the realities of a big city.

"Hatikvah," Israel's national anthem, describes the country as the "land of Zion *and* Jerusalem." The ideal can become real. As Rabbi Roland B. Gittelsohn writes: "To survive and develop creatively, a civilization must have a locus, a laboratory or hot-house, if you will, where it can be the primary culture of its people, where new strands and strains may be tested and refined." Israel is the lab for cultivating Jewish ideals, and Jerusalem is a place to dream.

❖ Notes

9 780827 614581